Words of Faith   *Prayers of* Ostad Elahi

Edited by Professor Bahram Elahi

Contents

Words of Faith

Prayers of Ostad Elahi

Introduction

Ostad Elahi was an inspired mystic, a monotheist philosopher,
and a compassionate, modest human being who founded
a school of spiritual philosophy on his answers to
the three existential questions of all time: "Where have I come
from? Why am I here? And where am I going?"
He called this school "The Path of Spiritual Perfection".
Even though, in the course of his life, Ostad Elahi addressed himself
only to a small circle of people who were close to him,
his universal teachings are not directed to any particular
group, but to human beings in general, irrespective of
religion, race, gender or nationality. A lifetime of unremitting
spiritual research, ascetic practice and intense personal
experience was at the root of Ostad Elahi's distinctive method
of demonstrating step by step, the practical stages of progress
towards spiritual perfection. He emphasised,
all along, that all his teachings were wholly rooted in personal
experience and that the essence of the lessons he gave was the
outcome of his own spiritual practice.
In demonstrating various aspects of his teachings, Ostad Elahi has not
allowed any major point to remain unexplained.
His revelations about the various levels of esoteric
understanding have the simplicity of a logical statement
describing deeply felt inner experiences.

Praying, in words and actions, is a major ingredient of Ostad Elahi's teachings. According to him, praying, in its true sense, is not merely an act of uttering a series of prepared words which, without heart-felt attention, would simply amount to a repetitive "clicking of the tongue". In its true devotional sense, praying signifies concentrating one's attention on God; and this in practice means total focusing of mind and feeling on God's presence, no matter where we are or what we are doing. A person aware of God's presence everywhere and in everything is in a state of constant devotion. For instance, when a student has the ultimate goal of spiritual perfection and sees God's presence as the guiding light in his daily life, then even his studying can be considered an act of devotion. Likewise, an employee who fulfils his duties conscientiously in the face of surrounding temptations is also engaged in a devotional process. A good illustration of this is provided by Ostad Elahi himself as he recalls his experience as a civil servant:

Before working for the government, I was unaware that my twelve years of ascetic practice had the same spiritual value as one year in the civil service. There, I did not give way to the many temptations that crossed my path.

This short book attempts to illustrate the emphasis placed on prayer in the teachings of Ostad Elahi. The first section contains a brief account of his life. The second section discusses his definition of prayer and its various stages. The third section contains sayings by Ostad Elahi dealing with the dimension of prayer in spiritual practice. The fourth section consists of three parts:

Ostad Elahi's Profession of Faith, originally written in verse, affirming the Oneness of God, which is the "point" on which religion, in its full sense, is based. That is what Ostad Elahi refers to when he says, "I found the Truth at the point of Unicity"

Quintessence of Religion, a prayer also originally written in verse, is the sum of many years of deliberation on religion.

A prayer by Ostad Elahi chosen for its comprehensiveness from among his ten prayers.

The fifth section contains a brief selection of Ostad Elahi's oral teachings, written down by his students. Each of these sayings could be considered a prayer in itself. The final section of this book contains a sample of Ostad Elahi's calligraphic exercises. This small book has been published on the occasion of the centenary of Ostad Elahi's birth and contains only a brief compilation restricted to the subjects of prayer and devotion. We hope, however, that it will contribute to making Ostad Elahi's thought better known to the public at large.

Bahram Elahi

Biography

Ostad Elahi (1895-1974)

Ostad Elahi was born on September 11, 1895 in Jeyhûnâbâd, a village in Western Iran. His father, Haj Nemat (1873-1920), was a prolific writer and mystical poet from a locally prominent family. Among his father's many writings was his major work, The Book of Kings of Truth [1] published by the Institut d'Iranologie headed by Henry Corbin [2], who described it as "a Bible unto itself".

During his childhood, Ostad Elahi led an ascetic, secluded life of rigorous spiritual discipline under his father's watchful supervision. He also received the classical education of that time, with a special focus on music, religion and ethical instruction as the foundation of all his training. It was during these formative years of his youth, which were completely devoted to contemplation and study, that he developed the basic foundations of his later philosophic and spiritual thinking.

At the age of twenty-four, he left his spiritual retreat, breaking with the local tradition that would have destined him to an entirely contemplative life. Having first worked at the Central Registry of Kermânshâh for a while, he eventually went to Tehran to study law. This radical change of life, he later explained, was necessary for him to deepen his thinking and to test his ethical and religious principles in the face of all the difficult demands of life in society. In 1933, he successfully completed his studies at the National School for Judicial Officials. His professional abilities and sense of equity and judgement were quickly recognised, and he was invariably entrusted with responsible assignments. For almost thirty years he was appointed to various positions throughout the country, sometimes as Public Prosecutor or Examining Magistrate, and eventually as Associate Justice and President of the National Court of Appeals.

1   *Shâhnâmeh-ye Haqiqat*, a Persian, mystical epic of 15,000 lines.
2   Henry Corbin (1903-1978), French philosopher, Professor at the Ecole Pratique des Hautes Etudes de Paris.

Throughout his legal career, Ostad Elahi continued to devote a great deal of time to personal studies and research, especially in the areas of philosophy and theology. Although little is known about the unfolding course of his thought during those years, it is clear that this period was extremely productive and filled with many experiences that richly nourished his studies and helped him to elaborate his later works. At the same time, spiritual music, which he had pursued since early childhood, continued to have an important place in his life. He was acknowledged by musical specialists to be a great virtuoso of the tanbûr (a Persian lute used in sacred music), enriching its repertoire through many original musical compositions and eventually attaining an extraordinary mastery of this instrument.

Ostad Elahi retired from the judiciary in 1957, and only then did he really begin to reveal his way of thought. He wrote two major scholarly works, learned and authoritative studies in their fields of religious thought and spirituality, as well as an extensive commentary on his father's work [3]. The practical spiritual aspect of Ostad Elahi's thought, on the other hand, was much more fully developed in the oral teaching and instruction which he shared with a few friends and students up until the end of his life in 1974. Two extensive volumes of his sayings and spiritual teachings have been published on the basis of notes written down by his students [4]. Those collected sayings bear the mark of profound spiritual inspiration, while they also reveal a penetrating understanding of human nature and a constant concern for intelligibility [5].

3   A commentary on *Haqq ol-Haqâyeq* by Ostad Elahi.
4   *Asâr ol-Haqq, (Traces of the Truth)*.
5   Some of Ostad Elahi's works are now being translated into French, English and other languages. A general summary of his ideas can be found in *The Path of Perfection*, by Bahram Elahi, Element Books, 1993.

Ostad Elahi's work is centered on the question of the nature of humankind, its place in the universe and its ultimate destination. Ostad's thought confirms the dual nature of human beings, as both spiritual and material, and reasserts the fundamental importance of our spiritual dimension. He reminds us that religion is what connects us with that spiritual dimension and ultimately with the Supreme Being. But the distinctive aspect of Ostad Elahi's thought lies in his definition of religion. As the essential core of the various revealed religions, Religion itself is presented as an ensemble of objective forms of understanding that can be called a "science". To the extent that Religion, in this deeper sense, is a science, it must also be universal. Thus, although Ostad Elahi's way of thinking was rooted in the Islamic tradition, it extends beyond the variations in religions due to history, culture and particular sensibilities. From this perspective, Religion can only claim to be objective if it is truly one and independent of any particular denomination or ritual. This way of thinking is not meant to deny the legitimacy of each religion, but rather to stress that their particular differences concern only their external and secondary aspects, while they are fundamentally one with regard to their essence and aim. The essential, universal dimension of religion is the means by which our primordial nature comes to fruition, thus fulfilling its essentially meta-physical destiny. This process of spiritual fulfilment or perfection is of funda-mental importance in Ostad Elahi's thought.

Human fulfilment requires something more than mere philosophical reflection. Religion, like any science, must necessarily be grounded in actual experience. That is why Ostad Elahi's theoretical teachings are inseparable from a practical, ethical dimension which is essentially based on the accomplishment of our intrinsic duties. The first of those duties is to understand our self as the basis for deeper knowledge and understanding. This self-understanding comes about through our striving to reach the right harmony and balance between the two opposing dimensions inherent in each human being. This striving is an active inner process that leads each individual seeker to be confronted with his or her own self through ongoing interaction with the surrounding environment and society.

On Prayer

On Prayer[*]

By nature, we, human beings tend to forget God, except when in
　　　　trouble. But if we are to avoid falling into a fatal slumber,
　　　　we have to remember God in more than just extreme
　　　　situations; that is why all religions have prescribed ritual
　　　　prayers, the purpose of which is to keep people from
　　　　forgetting God.
The essential goal of prayer, therefore, is to enable us to turn
　　　　our attention to God and come closer to Him.
　　　　From this perspective, it becomes possible to understand why
　　　　religious prescriptions such as fasting, charity or altruism
　　　　may be considered as 'prayers' in themselves, enabling us
　　　　to get closer to God.
When praying, we have to purify our intention and, in a state of true
　　　　humility, open our heart and speak to God. We should ask for
　　　　His grace and for the power to carry out His commands while
　　　　following the straight path. We may ask Him to protect us
　　　　against the temptations of the imperious self and shield us
　　　　against any source of evil. In feeling God's presence and
　　　　placing all our hope in Him, we must strive to fortify our faith
　　　　in His power over everything. Moreover, we must consider
　　　　as insignificant everything good we may have done and
　　　　expect nothing in return, either in this world or the next.
In the elementary stage of prayer, we may express certain wishes.
　　　　This enables us to become acquainted with God while
　　　　strengthening our confidence and preparing the way for
　　　　the next stages. In the upper stages, however, we should avoid
　　　　praying for the fulfilment of our wishes, for if fulfilled,
　　　　the equivalent amount will be deducted from our spiritual
　　　　savings. We must surrender to God's will and therefore try

---

[*]　Adapted from *The Path of Perfection*, by Dr. Bahram Elahi, Ch. 38. Passages in italics are translated
　　from *Bohrân ol-Haqq*, by Ostad Elahi, Ch. 18.

to be satisfied with whatever God decides for us as He is the only One Who knows what is truly in our interest. We may ask God to guide us in His way and help us accomplish His will: this is in fact the best of prayers. The prayer of the worshipper who loves God is but a means of drawing near to Him. In this state, the worshipper loves God only for God and adores Him not out of any particular interest, but solely because He is worthy of being adored.

The Four Stages of Prayer

There are four stages of prayer, each relating to a different level of spiritual maturity:

The first stage is that of praying with the mind in the physical dimension. This kind of prayer is practised differently by the followers of different religions. […] It results in keeping the worshipper from doing base and illicit deeds. […]

This is the exoteric stage, which is based on obedience; the adherents of different religions practice different ritual prayers in the course of which they try to concentrate on God and drive distracting thoughts away. At this stage, the words have only a formal and conceptual meaning for the worshipper. The verbal, ritual prayer may be likened to an answer to God; it does not always lead to a communication of the heart with God, but it is the stage that precedes it.

In the second stage, praying is free from physical, verbal and ritual constraints. The prayer rises from the heart and results in heartfelt attention and spiritual insight. It expands and rises higher than the prayer of the first stage. […] It releases the worshipper from worldly attachments, material temptations and physical passions. […]

At this stage, the worshipper reaches an angelic state, relieved from
the necessity of struggling with the interference of passing
thoughts in order to concentrate on God, and is, instead,
drawn towards the spiritual world as though by a magnet.
The prayer and the divine words begin to have a deeper and
truer meaning and resonance, penetrating the whole
of the worshipper's being. The body and the angelic soul
communicate; one feels in a state of grace with the sensation
of coming close to the spiritual world and being
in the shadow of the Divine Presence. This is the beginning
of the spiritual awakening.

In the third stage, the prayer rises from the level of the heart to that of
the soul. Free from the constraints of matter and form, the soul
becomes a traveller in the metaphysical dimension.
This is the stage of spiritual understanding and the knowledge
of the self, where faith is transformed into certainty.

At this stage, the soul leaves the body behind and enters the realm
of pure spirituality. It is a world of unimaginable wonders
where the soul freely moves about, contemplating its
beauties. The presence of God becomes more distinct and one
becomes fully aware of one's self. Those who reach this stage
become fully certain of the truth upon which they have based
their faith. In knowing themselves, they come to know God.

In the fourth stage, the soul, like a drop of water, vanishes into the limitless
ocean of Unicity. This is where the soul finally joins its divine
origin. This is the stage of Truth.

At this stage, the soul is linked with the world of the 'Real Truth' in the
proximity of God. Those who reach that stage are so totally
absorbed by the feeling of wonder and happiness that they
forget everything, even their own self. Their souls are linked
with God and they contemplate nothing but God alone.

After that, there remain three more levels before reaching Perfection.

A Few Short Sayings About Prayer

This section contains sayings by Ostad Elahi dealing with the dimension of prayer in spiritual practice. Some of these sayings are brief answers to questions asked by students, and others are extracts from his lessons about the various levels of praying.

Attention to God is the highest act of devotion.

Intention is the main thing in praying. No matter what your religion or
what language you speak, as soon as your attention is focused
on God, your prayer is accepted.

To be effective, prayer must combine action, attention and recollection.

The act of prayer is not limited to a particular time and place: wherever
and whenever you are with God, God is with you.

The effect of prayer depends on the time, the intention, the sincerity
and the feelings of the person who is praying.

The prayer of a true servant of God consists of praise for Him, pleading
for His help and submitting to His will, no matter what words
are used or what manner is employed.

Collective praying, provided all the worshippers are of one heart,
is always more effective than individual praying.

Whenever and wherever the attention to God comes, hold on to it.
It may come in the most crowded street and it may come
at any time.

Praying must not be motivated by fear, hypocrisy, or greed;
       it should spring from pure intention, aiming at nothing
       but God's satisfaction.

Why are there repetitions in prayers? Because repetition eventually
       results in concentrated attention which in turn strengthens
       the capacity for attention.

Even one moment of attention to God, if rooted in full faith
       and complete certainty, is instantly registered and added
       to one's spiritual savings.

Do not let yourself be deceived by the imperious self when it says
       "Now that you can't pray as you should, you'd better not pray
       at all!" This is typical of the imperious self; it shouldn't be
       listened to.

Every intimate discourse with God is registered in the spiritual world
       and stays there forever. Likewise, every time your thoughts
       wander, it is reflected there.

Praying for one's parents and for people of faith is a service rendered
       to society, for it is like sowing the seeds of goodness.

God has allowed us to pray for other people. It is indeed most
praiseworthy and amounts to giving them a helping hand.

While praying, in order to achieve attention to God, think that you are
addressing a large assembly: you must feel every word before
you speak it, and concerning humility and submission,
imagine that you stand before God and He is listening to you.

A moment of heart-felt attention to God is equal to a year
of routine devotion.

I begin my midday prayer when the two hands of my watch indicate
noontime. I begin the evening prayer at the official time
for sunset, and I link the night and dawn prayers so that
the last word of my night prayer is followed by the first word
of the dawn prayer.

How to pray to God to grant the requests of others: "O God, 'so and so'
has a request; as is our religious duty, we beseech You to grant
that request, if it be Your will".

Praying, even reluctantly, is better than not praying at all.

You should all reach the level where praying, far from being
       an obligation, gives you joy and elation.

It is our duty to pray for people in general.

A heart-felt prayer leaves a trace that lasts for a thousand years.

The best time for praying is just before dawn. O, to be awake
       at that hour and, in a state of submission, concentrating
       one's attention on God!

Wherever you hear the Name of God, respect it, welcome it, and be
       blessed by it – never mind who speaks it or where it is spoken.
       Do not set yourself apart.

When we say "O God of Abraham!", it means that we invoke God
       in the same purity of heart and with the same love
       as Abraham did.

The highest form of prayer is to guide others towards the right path,
       that is, the straight, middle course, away from both extremes.

God has allowed praying fo other pe
people. It is indeed most laudable an
and amounts to giving them a helpfull
hand. God has allowed praying for oth
other people. It is indeed most laudab
laudable and amounts to giving them a
a helpfull hand- God has allowed pray
praying for other people. It is indeed m
most laudable and amounts to giving th
them a helpfull hand God has allowed
praying for other people It is indeed
most laudable and amounts to giving th
them a helpfull hand. God has allowed
praying for other people It is indeed m
most laudable and amounts to giving th

Charles Hossein Zenderoudi 95

Prayers

Profession of Faith

O God I attest, O God I attest.

With absolute certainty, I thus attest

I come from *Yâr*[1] and to Him I shall return.

For *Yâr* is God, the Unique, the Sustainer

Creator of all creatures, Necessary Being

Originator of both the existent and the possible

In His praise, I call to mind the invocation of Unicity

For so does my conscience bid me:

"Say God is but One" – this in earnest

Also intoning: "God is sovereign"

He was not born and gave no birth

And none is equal to Him.

I do attest that the same unique God

Is my creator, as witness my existence.

I walk the path of Truth

[…]

And the Truth I found at the point of Unicity

[…]

At the end of my prayer, O Lord

I beseech You to forgive all my sins, my misdeeds and iniquities.

Out of your magnanimity, cast a glance at your servant

Out of your bounty, give shelter to this poor creature

Rest my parents' souls

Absolve my sins and those of all believers.

Illuminate our hearts with the light of faith

Bring joy to our souls with the light of *Ali*[2].

---

1   *Yâr* is one of the names of God, meaning friend, companion, helper.
2   *Ali* is one of the names of God.

Quintessence of Religion

If the essence of religion is what you seek
Here are the principles and tenets you should embrace:

First, put your faith in God
The Unique, the Peerless, the Invisible
One without associates, who was not born and will not die.

Second, consider as good every creature whatever and at all times.
Since no being is bad in origin:
It's the deed that's bad, not the doer.
Strive, therefore, to combat bad deeds.
As for those known for their goodness
You owe them respect, whatever their status.

Third, everywhere and at all times
Whatever is deemed good by the wise
Whatever leads to order and peace for people
And comes from the Source of Truth
Practice it for yourself and for others
And stay away from what is counter to it.

Beyond that, you may embrace any religion
Not opposed to these principles
Provided you practice its commandments in good faith.

After much research, Nour 'Ali found this to be
Truly the quintessence of all religions.

Prayer

O God, the Unique, the Peerless, the Living, the Almighty
O Necessary Being, Creator of all creatures, encompassing all
O the most Merciful, the most Munificent
"The Lord of both worlds, the Compassionate, the Merciful
The Sovereign of the Day of Judgment
The One, the Self-Subsistent
The One who was not born and gave no birth".
It is You that I adore
And to You I turn for help.

I plead with You
And then I plead with You again
In the name of all the beings that exist or may exist
Those of the past, present and future
From the beginning, till the end of time
Those who are sacred, dear and close to You
And whose prayers are answered by You.
I beseech You to forgive the countless sins
I have committed throughout my life
And to keep me always on the right path
The path that would lead me to You
And about which it is said:
"Guide us on the straight path

The path of those on whom You have bestowed Your bounty
And not that of those who have incurred Your wrath
Or those who have gone astray".

So, preserve me in such a way
That You'd be fully satisfied with me in both worlds.
Do not ever let me, for any reason
Commit, desire or confront anything that is contrary to Your satisfaction.

Also, as is my religious duty
I plead for Your mercy, grace, goodness and blessing
For the souls of my parents
And all believers
And indeed all creatures.

Amen.

Prayer Sayings

This section contains a brief selection of Ostad Elahi's oral teachings, written down by his students. Each saying here is in itself a short prayer, relayed by Ostad Elahi in the course of discussions with his students. In quoting them out of context, we have relied upon the reader to reach for deeper meanings underlying the short phrases, and thus get a feeling of the intimate relation that can exist between God and human beings.

O Unique God,
Bless me with the happiness of knowing You.

O God, let Your satisfaction be my guideline,
For therein lies the Truth.

O God,
We ask You to grant us only Your satisfaction.
We want no happiness other than remembering You
At all times and having our hearts filled with the light of faith.
Amen.

I worship You,
O God,
And want nothing in return.
Give me whatever You will,
And withhold whatever You will.
Only protect me from resorting to flattery.

O Mighty God,
Preserve us from the guiles of this world!

I beseech You,
O God,
To transform our faith into certainty
So that we shall no longer be prey to doubts,
Temptations and the promptings of the tenebrous self!

Protect us,
O God,
From the evils of our imperious self.

O God,
Keep us by force of destiny,
From wanting anything but Your satisfaction,
And protect us from whatever is not to Your satisfaction.

God,
I beseech You to watch over me.

O God,
Keep us from losing our faith.

O God,
Do not put us on trial,
For we are not worthy of being tried.

O God,
Keep us from becoming conceited,
Or being misled,
Or condemned to ignorance.

O God,
Grant us the grace not to hurt or wrong any creature,
Especially any human being,
And let all creatures be kind to us.

O God,
Give me the happiness and blessing of doing
That which would give You satisfaction and rejecting everything
That is contrary to Your satisfaction.
I seek Your satisfaction for its own sake,
Not for receiving anything in return from You.

O God,
Let us not forget You,
Lest we be misled by the appearances of this world.

May God always help us to be good to others;
And if someone has harmed us,
We wish that no harm may come to that person.

O God,
Help us always to be of benefit to others.

O God,
I serve You and obey Your commands
So that You may be satisfied with me.

O God,
Lead us always on the straight path.

O God and Master,
May we succeed in adopting Your ways in every respect.

O God,
Only Your Mercy is greater than my sins!

O Creator of the Universe,
We are made from Your Breath,
So what is in You is also in us.
We will not demean ourselves by asking You for anything
But Your satisfaction.

O God,
Will we ever attain the "perfection" that knows no bounds
And does not result in tedium and decay…
Where one is in an everlasting state of elation
And every passing moment brings on an even greater pleasure.

I was always deeply moved when my father would say, while praying:

O God,
Everyone is asleep but You!

O Creator of all creatures,
Encompassing all,
You are manifest everywhere;
May my life be given up to You.

O God,
May everyone ever to be born in this household
Be blessed with faith!

O God,
I place myself and my family in Your hands;
Protect us from the corrupt environment of these times.

Lead us to the path where we will be guided
By Your will and not ours.
O God,
You are Just,
But You are also Merciful and Compassionate.
If You choose to apply Your Justice to us,
Then woe unto us;
But we pray that You will treat us with Mercy and Compassion.

O God,
As a matter of religious duty and human feeling,
I ask Your mercy,
Grace and blessing for the souls of my parents,
For all the people of faith,
And indeed for all other beings.
O Sovereign of both worlds,
If it be Your Will,
Answer my prayer.
Amen.

May God never let man's lot be decided by man.

O God,
If it be Your will,
Make it possible that no one will be in need of pity.

O God,
Never let me be in a position where I would inspire pity.

O God may I never be dependent on anything,
Even to the point that my hands will never be
In need of each other.

O God,
Torment me for thousands of years in this world
Rather than punishing me for one minute in the next.

O God,
Save us from the two incurable diseases of doubt and pride!

O God,
By Your grace,
Make it possible for us to pass through
The thousand taxing stages of liberation.

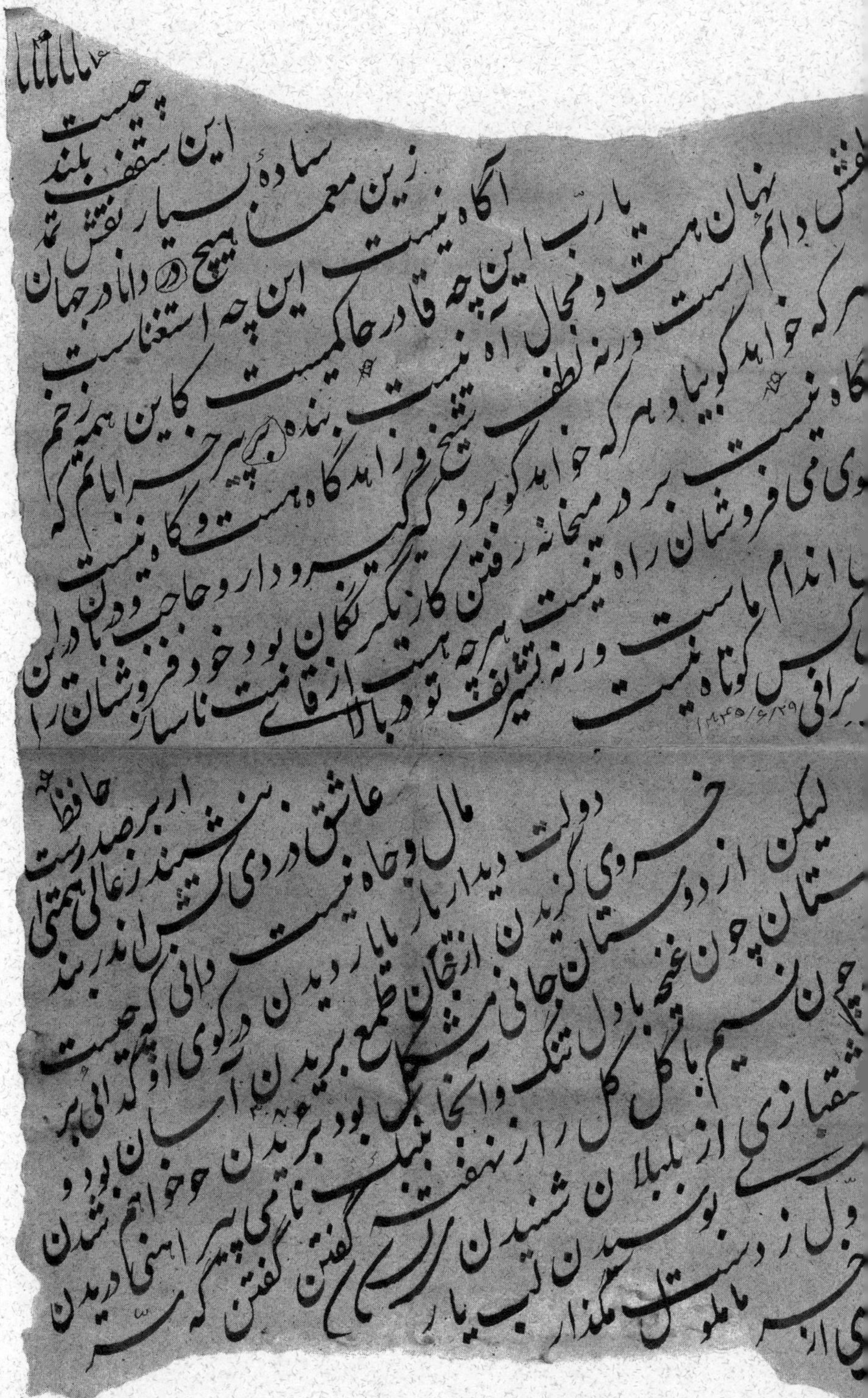

Manuscripts:
Pages 44-47; Exercises in Calligraphy by Ostad Elahi, mystical poems 1966. Indian ink on packing paper, recto and verso.

Paintings:
Charles Hossein Zenderoudi, from the prayers of Ostad Elahi.
Page 25; *Helping Hand*, 1995. Acrylic and ink on paper, 30×30 cm.
Page 26; *Give me Happiness*, 1995. Acrylic and ink on paper, 30×30 cm.
Page 35; *Merciful*, 1995. Acrylic and ink on paper, 30×30 cm.
Page 36; *Always*, 1995. Acrylic and ink on paper, 30×30 cm.

ISBN : 2 - 9113 - 3102 - 2

Dépot légal : Août 1995
© Robert Laffont

Achevé d'imprimer : Août 1995

Peintures : © Hossein Zenderoudi, Spadem

Mise en page : © Rudi Meyer, Spadem

Photogravure et impression : La Chapelle Montligeon

Imprimé en France